Play
with a purpose

with birds and flowers

BrambleKids

INTRODUCTION

YOUNG AND CREATIVE

With a focus on birds and flowers, these activities improve children's understanding of the outdoor world. Understanding the parts of a flower, and recognising different birds, both flying and in the water, form part of early teaching. The making of models using these topics as inspiration provides a proven source of artistic creativity and skills in basic engineering.

All these learning elements are an ideal preparation and support for school-based learning.

NEW FROM OLD

The theme-based activities in this book afford valuable opportunities to inspire children to learn about RECYCLING. Many of the materials needed are everyday items used in the home that children can turn into something exciting!

These educational crafts will motivate children to keep and reuse many items, such as empty yoghurt pots, jars, kitchen roll tubes and newspapers. They will also teach how to correctly recycle any waste from all activities where appropriate and explain why it is important to do so.

Take care!

Some of the activities in this book will require adult supervision. Encourage children to use scissors and pointed utensils with care and in a safe manner, further helping to build their skills and confidence.

CONTENTS

Flower Projects

1	You will need	6-7
2	Make a Leaf Print	8
3	Make a Potato Print	9
4	Make a Sunflower	10-11
5	Make a Seed Mat	12
6	Make Leaf Tiles	13
7	Make a Toadstool	14-15
8	Make a 3D Tree	16-17
9	Make a Cactus	18-19
10	Make Tissue Paper Flowers	20-21
11	Make a Floppy Flower	22-23
12	Make a Window Box	24
13	Make Flower Garlands	24-25
14	Make a String Print	26
15	Make a String Flower and a String Tree	27
16	Make Pressed Flower Cards	28-29
17	Make a Palm Tree	30
18	Bake some Flower Tarts	31

Bird Projects

19	A Papier Mâché Owl	32-33
20	Make Decorated Eggs	34
21	Make a Line of Ducks	35
22	Make a Fluffy Chick	36-37
23	Make a Nest for your Chick	38
24	Make a Hatching Chick	39
25	Make a Flying Bird	40-41
26	Make a Peacock	42
27	Make a Bird Mobile	43
28	Make a Curly Bird	44-45
29	Make Swimming Swans	46
30	Make a Rocking Penguin	47

Development Links

Physical Skills

* **Development of fine motor skills**
  All these activities require the movement of hands and fingers. These in turn will involve the use and practice of fine motor skills and the general improvement of muscle control and strength. Developing these skills will extend into everyday activities such as washing and dressing.

* **Increase in dexterity**
  All these activities require manual dexterity. With practice and time, finer artistic skills will increase.

* **Improvements in hand-eye coordination**
  These activities require keen hand-eye coordination and such practice will support the development in further areas such as sports.

Intellectual Skills

* **Promotion of innovation and creativity**
  These activities offer children opportunities to create something new. This will encourage them to think differently and to innovate ideas.

* **Development of problem-solving skills**
  These activities require children to follow instructions and be resourceful. Encouraging them to work out where they may have gone wrong through discussion will support them in later life.

* **Enhancement of decision-making skills**
  Solving artistic challenges will promote correct and effective decision-making abilities. This will improve their ability to face other problems.

* **Improvement in memory**
  These activities require children to use and develop their visualising skills. Visualising complex designs will help improve memory.

* **Improvements in visual processing**
  These activities require children to identify patterns and colours that will naturally develop visual processing skills. This cognitive development is very important in early years.

Emotional and Social Skills

✱ Improvements in self-esteem
Encouraging children in these activities will boost their self-esteem. With each completed activity, children will feel a sense of achievement. Creating something allows children to feel in control and confident in themselves.

✱ Confident expression of self
Artistic activities encourage children to express themselves and your praise and encouragement will give them the confidence to do so. Children can channel negative and positive energy into these activities.

✱ Encouragement of creativity
Although instructed, all of the activities allow children to use their imagination and turn it into something productive. This will nurture artistic talents and self-esteem.

✱ Improvements in working with others
Encouraging children to work on these activities with their peers, whether they create a project together or simply support one another, will hugely develop their social skills and abilities. Interacting with other children with the same interests, or working together to overcome differences, will allow for friendships to develop.

✱ Strengthening of bonds
Working together with the child on these activities as a parent or teacher will strengthen your bond. Company will promote the children's enjoyment and engagement with the activity.

1 You will need

This book uses things that are usually found around the house or even things that might normally get thrown away. There are just a few things that might need to be purchased especially.

scissors

ruler

paints

sticky tape

string

paintbrushes

cardboard or kitchen roll

balls of wool

needle and thread

toothpicks or cocktail sticks

TIP

A note about glue

There are three types of glue we have used: school glue or paste, PVA and glue sticks. If you are sticking paper and card together, then a glue stick is the best one to use. School glue is best for papier mâché and PVA is best for heavier things, hard surfaces and wool. You can also use PVA as a kind of varnish. If you paint it onto a surface, it will go shiny when it dries.

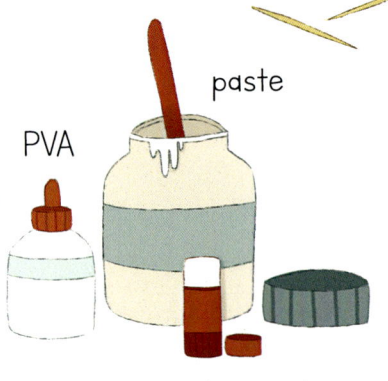

paste

PVA

glue stick

How to Make Papier Mâché

Papier mâché is a really fun material to make. It's a mix of paper and glue, or flour and water paste, which hardens when it dries. You can build up layers of paper to mould a vase or a bowl, or scrunch up torn newspaper pieces to make the shape of an animal or person.

Papier mâché takes a long time to dry, so wait before you paint or decorate it.

Things to Remember

If you are covering an object to make a papier-mâché mould, it's best to cover the object in cling film to start with. Use school glue or flour mixed with water into a thick paste. The more layers you add, the firmer your shape will be. Make sure the paper is really soggy with paste for the best results. It won't be waterproof.

sticks or twigs

balloons

cooking oil

coloured paper

seeds and rice

plaster powder

paper plates

bowl and old spoon

2 Make a Leaf Print

You will need
Thickly mixed paints
Paintbrushes
Sheet of white paper
Newspaper
Different leaves

1 Take one leaf and paint evenly over the side that has the leaf veins sticking up.

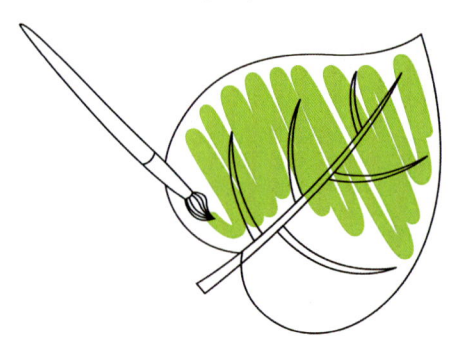

2 Place it carefully paint side down on the white paper then put the newspaper carefully over the leaf.

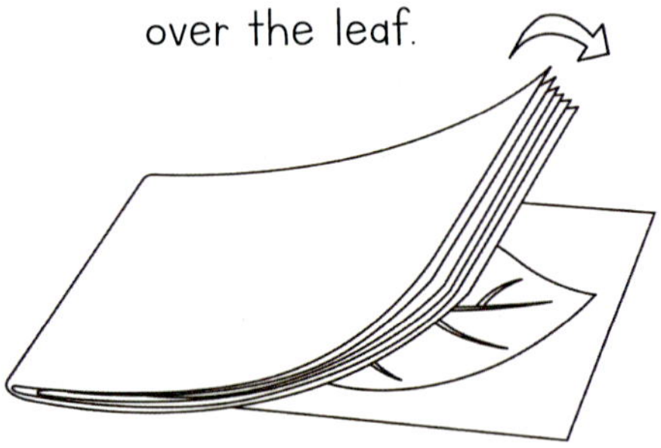

3 Rub slowly and firmly over the newspaper to print your leaf.

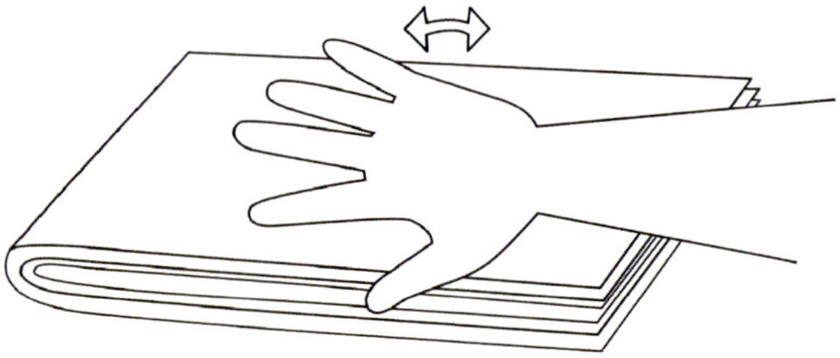

TIP
Repeat with lots of different leaves and perhaps some ferns.

3. Make a Potato Print

You will need

- A large potato
- A kitchen knife
- Paper
- Paints
- Paintbrushes
- Sheet of newspaper or kitchen roll
- Pen

1. Cut the potato in half and blot the surface on the newspaper.

2. Draw your shape on the face of the potato. Draw a simple shape that is easy to cut round. Then very carefully, cut away the background so only your shape is left raised.

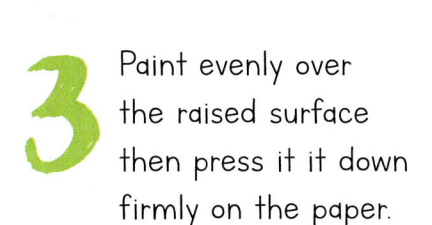

3. Paint evenly over the raised surface then press it it down firmly on the paper.

4 Make a Sunflower

You will need

A large plate
A small saucer
Cardboard
Pencil
Yellow, black and brown tissue paper
Scissors
PVA glue

1 Draw a circle on the cardboard by drawing round the small saucer. Then cut it out.

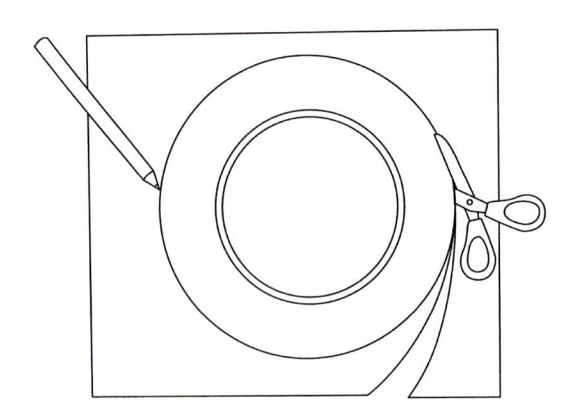

2 Put two sheets of yellow tissue paper together and draw a circle by drawing around the large plate. Cut them out.

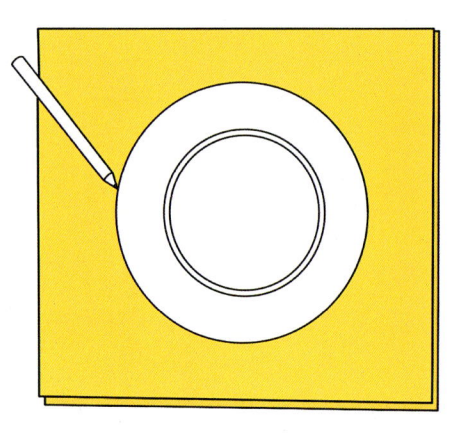

3 Cut petal shapes around the edges of the tissue circles.

4 Glue the tissue circles together, making sure the petals overlap to create a nice flower. Then glue the cardboard circle on top.

5 Scrunch up the other coloured tissue paper into little balls and glue them to the centre of your flower.

TIP When you have finished you could tape some string to the back and hang it up.

5 Make a seed mat

You will need

Plaster powder
A bowl for mixing
An old spoon
A jar lid
Dried peas, lentils, beans, pasta and sunflower seeds

1 Mix a small quantity of plaster powder into a thick paste. Spoon it into the lid and smooth it off.

2 Carefully arrange your dried seeds to make a flower pattern. Press them gently into the plaster.

3 Leave to dry.

6 Make Leaf Tiles

You will need

Some leaves
Plaster powder
Bowl for mixing
Acrylic paints, gold or silver
   is nice if you have it
A square or rectangular lid
   from a lunch box or tray
Cling film
PVA glue

1 Line the tray or lid with the cling film and leave plenty outside so that you can pull it out afterwards.

2 Mix the powder with water into a very thick paste. Put the plaster in the lid or tray and smooth it off.

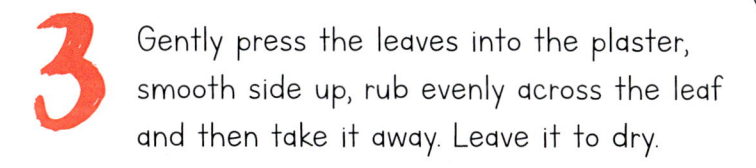

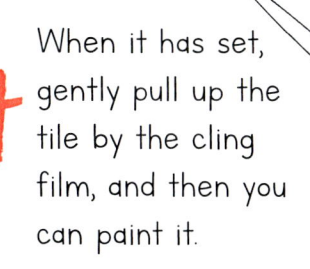

3 Gently press the leaves into the plaster, smooth side up, rub evenly across the leaf and then take it away. Leave it to dry.

4 When it has set, gently pull up the tile by the cling film, and then you can paint it.

TIP

If you want your tile to be shiny you can paint it with PVA glue.

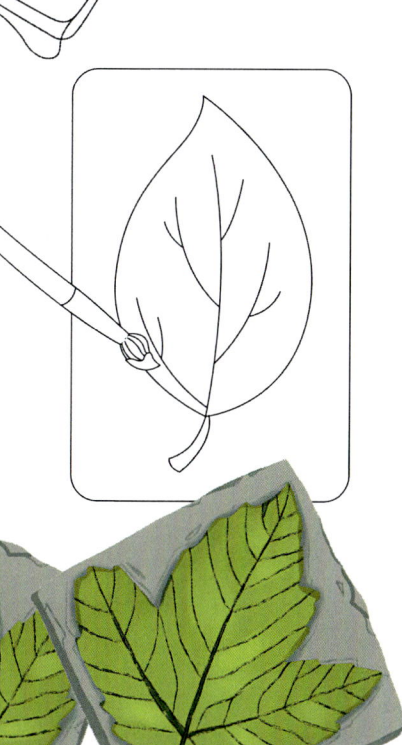

7 Make a Toadstool

You will need

A small bowl
Newspaper
Cling film
A bowl of water
A paint brush
School glue
Paints
Cardboard tube from kitchen roll

1 Rip up the newspaper and soak in water.

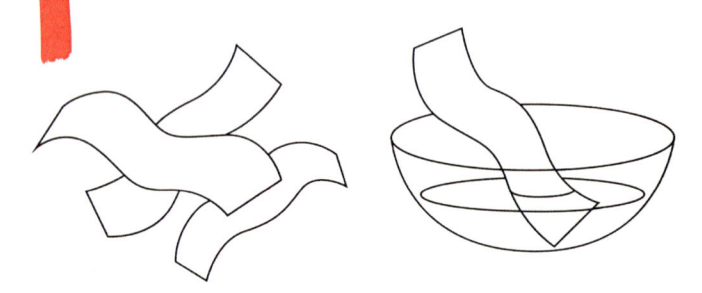

2 Cover the outside of the bowl with the cling film to stop the paper from sticking.

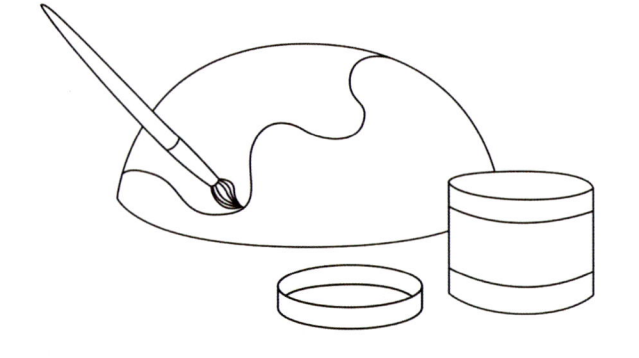

3 Paint the outside of the bowl with paste. Then stick pieces of the wet paper to the bowl, making sure you don't leave any gaps.

4 Stick on another layer. Repeat this process about ten times. Leave it to dry.

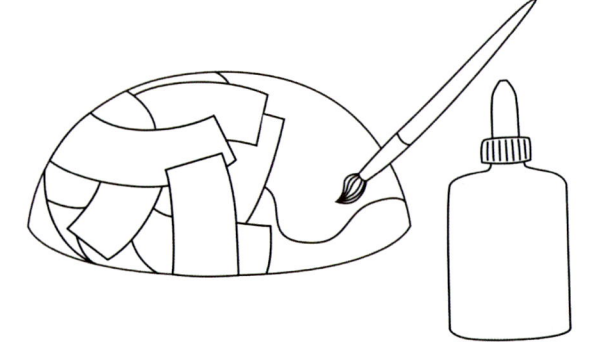

5 When it has dried completely, gently ease it off the bowl.

Paint the kitchen roll tube and the the top of the toadstool and put them together to form your toadstool.

8 Make a 3D Tree

You will need

Pens   Scissors   A piece of paper   Green tissue or lightweight paper   Glue

1 Take your piece of paper and fold it in half and then in half again.

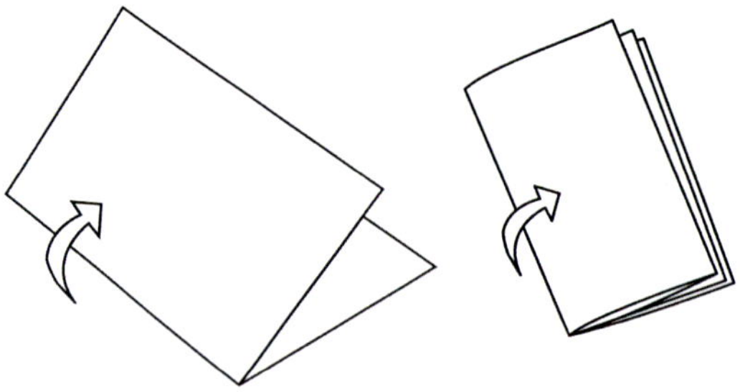

2 Draw a tree on the top part but make sure that the trunk spreads out to cover the bottom of the paper. This will form the base for your tree.

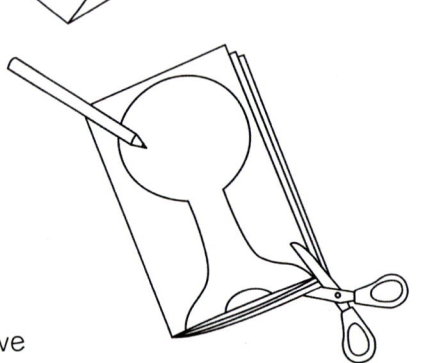

3 Carefully cut out the tree so that you have four trees that are all the same shape.

4 Colour in the trees with the pens. You could do them all the same or you could do one for each season.

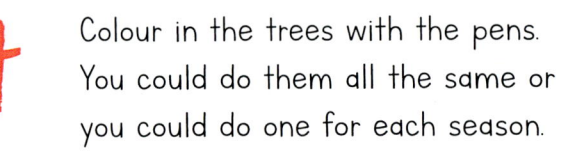

5 Take the first tree and fold it in half with the drawing on the inside. Put some glue on the half that faces you. Take the next tree, fold it in half and stick it directly onto the first tree. Stick all the trees together in this way until you get to the end.

6 Cut out leaf shapes and stick them onto the branches. Use light weight paper for the leaves so the branches don't sag from the weight.

9 Make a Cactus

You will need

A tube from a kitchen roll
Newspaper
Sticky tape
Glue
Toothpicks
Paints
A brush
A small plant pot with some pebbles in

1 Scrunch up the newspaper into balls and stick them to the roll. Use lots of glue. Try and make it nice and fat at the top to make a good cactus shape.

2 Glue strips of newspaper over the top to smooth it off. Leave it to dry.

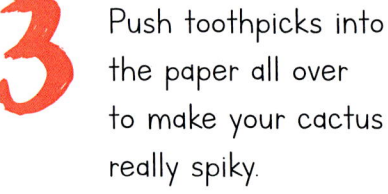

3 Push toothpicks into the paper all over to make your cactus really spiky.

18

Now you can paint it and decorate it. When it's dry, put it in the plant pot using the pebbles to help it stand up.

10 Make Tissue Paper Flowers

You will need
Coloured tissue paper
Scissors
String
Sticky tape
Paper drinking straws

You can hang up your flowers or you can tape them onto a straw. Experiment by painting them different colours.

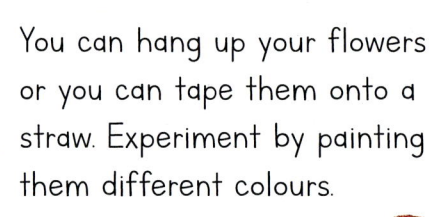

1 Cut the paper handkerchiefs into lengths about 10 centimetres (cm) x 20 cm.

2 Put four sheets together on top of each other. Then fold them back and forth to make a fan.

3 Tie a piece of string around the middle of the paper using a strong knot.

4 Very gently pull the layers of paper apart on both sides to make your flower.

11 Make A Floppy Flower

You will need
Coloured paper
Scissors
Sticky tape
A stick

1 Fold the piece of paper in half. Cut strips in the paper starting on the side with the fold. Don't go all the way across, stop about 1 cm from the edge.

2 Unfold it and then gently bring the two long sides together the opposite way you folded it the first time.

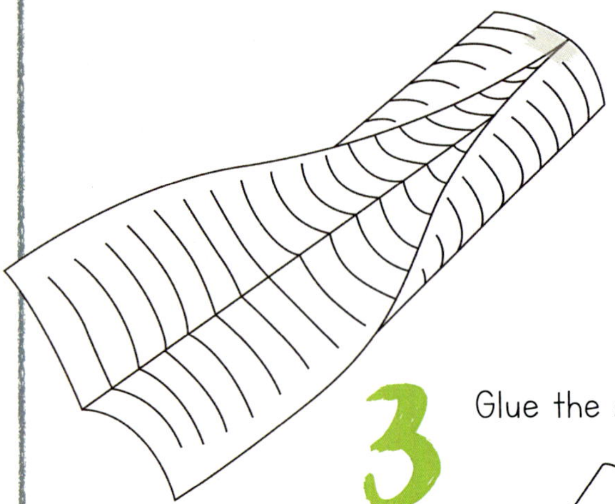

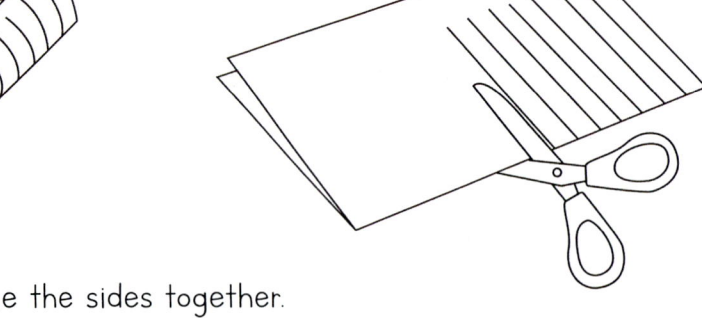

3 Glue the sides together.

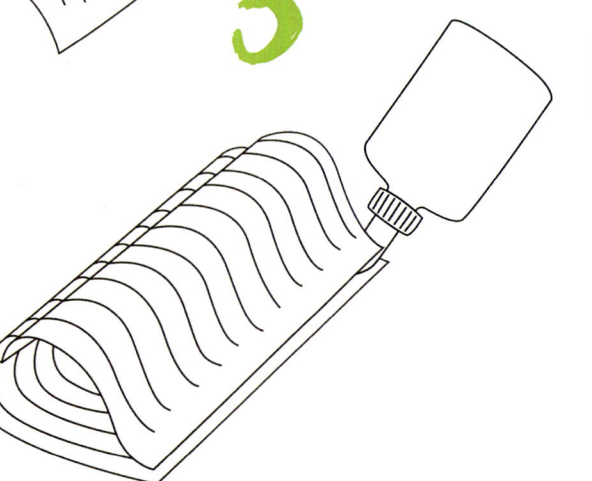

4 Tape one end of the paper to the stick and then to begin to roll it onto the stick.

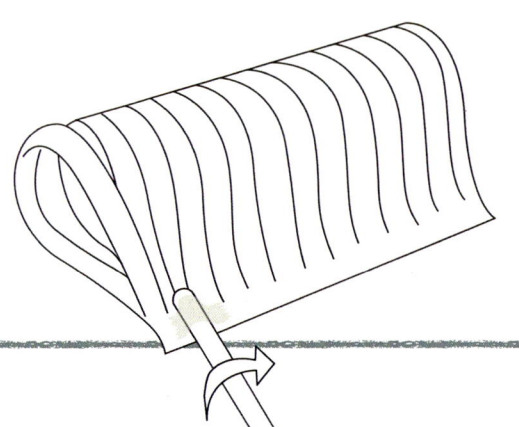

5 When you get to the end, fix it with a bit of tape.

Fluff up the petals.

TIP

If you want an extra big flower, make another one and stick it on the stick just underneath the first.

12 Make a window box

You will need
A firm cardboard box
Green or brown wrapping paper
Scissors
Sticky tape

1 Cover the cardboard box with wrapping paper and secure with tape.

2 Wedge the sticks of the flowers from pages 20, 21, 22 and 23, or any other ones you've made on sticks, into the top of your window box.

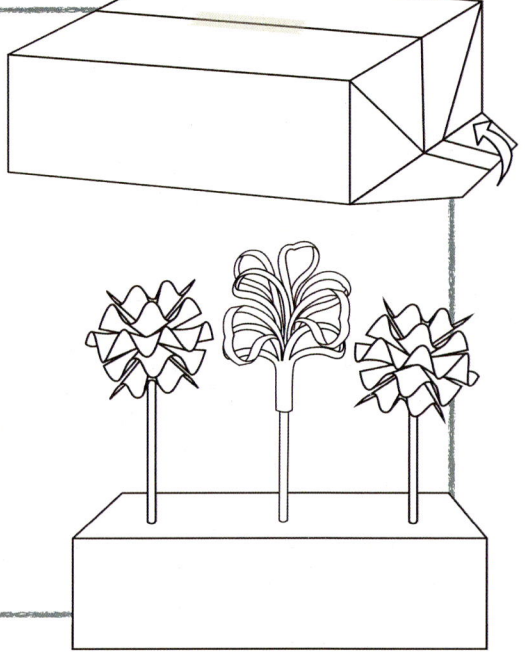

13 Make flower garlands

You will need
Coloured tissue paper
Scissors
Sticky tape
Plastic coated garden wire

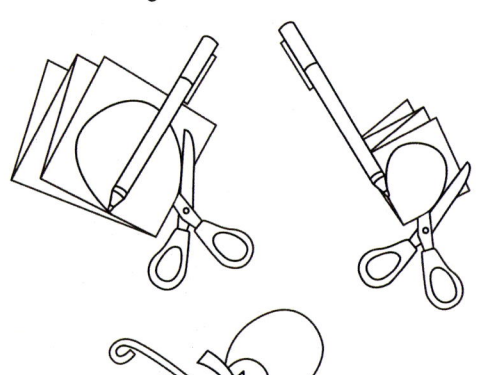

1 Cut squares of tissue paper. Fold them in four. Draw a petal shape on the front fold. Then cut round the shape and open it out.

2 Cut smaller squares and fold and cut them in the same way. Place them in the centre of the first flower.

3 Poke a length of garden wire carefully through the centre of each flower and curl it so it won't slip out.

25

14 Make a String Print

You will need
A small square of very stiff card or block of thin wood
Thick string
Scissors
PVA glue
Paints and paintbrush
Sheet of white paper

1 Cut a length of string about 30 cm long. Glue one end of it to the cardboard or wood, putting just a dab of glue on the string.

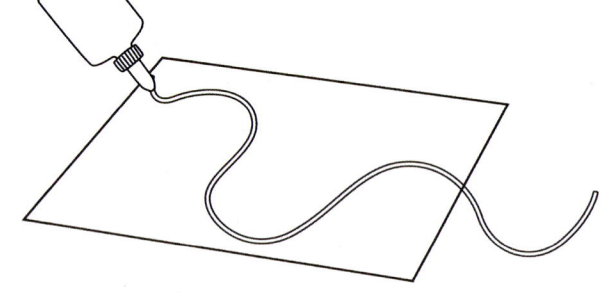

2 Slowly glue the rest of the string onto the board, coiling ad weaving it into a pattern or shape. Let it dry. This is your string print block.

3 Cover the string with paint and press it down on the paper to make a coloured string print.

Repeat the print for a completely patterned sheet of paper.

15 Make a String Flower

You will need
Card
Pen
Scissors
A bottle top
Wool
Tape
Ruler

1 Draw a circle on the card. Use a bottle top to draw petals all the way around the rim and then cut it out.

2 Tape a piece of wool to the back of the card. Then bring it over to the front and wind it round and round. You can experiment with lots of different patterns.

3 When you have finished, tape the wool to the back but leave a long piece so that you can hang it up.

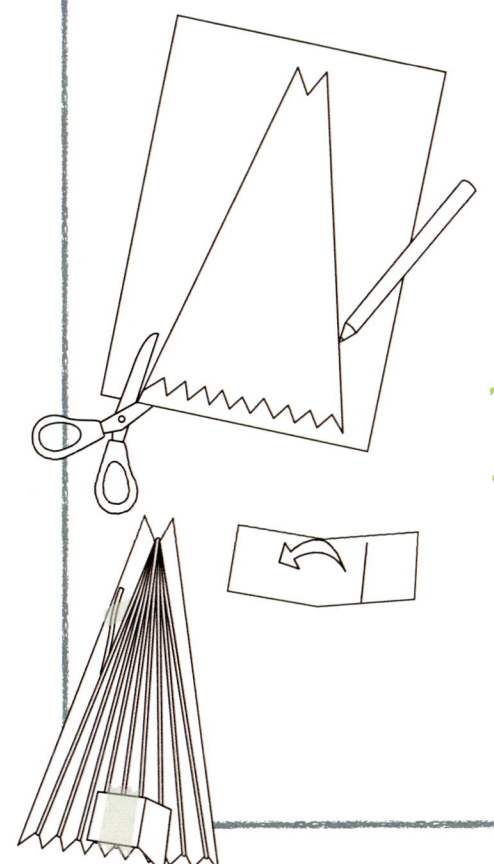

and a String Tree

1 Use the ruler to draw a triangle on the card and cut it out. Cut a notch in the top and lots of notches all along the bottom of the triangle.

2 Cut a long piece of wool and tape it to the back of the tree. Bring it to the front and wind it around the tree between the notches. Tie on more wool at the back if needed. When you have covered the triangle, tape the end of the wool to the back.

3 Cut a piece of card in a rectangle. Fold it half and tape one half to the bottom of the tree at the back. Now it can stand up.

16 Make Pressed Flower Cards

You can use any sort of flowers for this as long as you check first that it is all right to pick them. Big petals are lovely if you can find them.

You will need

Flowers
Card
Glue
Newspaper and heavy books

1 Press the flowers very carefully by opening out their petals and laying them between sheets of blotting paper or newspaper.

2 Leave them pressed under heavy books for at least a week.

3 Arrange them carefully and glue them in place on to your card.

29

17 Make a Palm Tree

You will need
Stiff green card
Scissors
Sticky tape

1 Cut the piece of card about 30 cm by 10 cm. Roll it up and secure it with tape.

2 Cut though all the thicknesses in fairly close lines. Do not cut quite as far as the base.

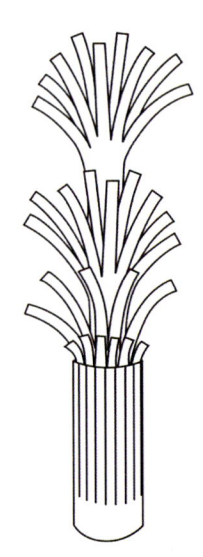

3 Pull the branches up from the centre of the roll. Fluff them up to make your palm tree really bushy.

18 Bake Some Flower Tarts

You will need

Kitchen scales
A bowl for mixing
Rolling pin
Shallow bun tray
Spoon and knife
Pastry cutter

250 g flour
125 g butter
1 egg
Jam

Cut the butter into small bits with the knife. Put the flour and butter in the bowl.

Use your fingertips to rub the butter and the flour together until it looks like breadcrumbs.

Add the egg, and mix it all together to form a dough. If it's a bit dry, add a little water.

Wrap it in cling film and leave it in the fridge for half an hour.

When it is cool, dust the table with flour and roll out the dough using the rolling pin.

Cut out circles with the pastry cutter and put them into the cups on the bun tray.

Spoon the jam into each cup.

Now cut lots of petal shapes in the pastry with the knife.

Overlap them around the edge of your tarts to make a flower. Leave a circle in the middle so that you can still see the jam.

Ask an adult to cook your flowers for about 15 minutes at 200° C. Jam gets vey hot in the oven so leave them to cool for a long time before gently removing them from the tray.

19 A Papier Mâché Owl

You will need

A balloon
Some cooking oil
Pieces of newspaper
Thin paste or glue
Some dried beans or rice
Paints
Paint brushes
Clear varnish
A pin

1 Blow up the balloon to the size you want and tie a knot in it. Then smear the balloon with oil.

2 Cover it with three to four layers of papier mâché, leaving the knot uncovered. Leave it to dry for 24 hours.

3 Pop the balloon with a pin and pull it carefully out of the dried papier mâché shape. Fill with enough dried beans or rice to steady it. Papier mâché over the hole and leave to dry.

4 Paint the owl. When the paint is dry, coat with clear varnish.

20 Make decorated eggs

You will need

Pencil
Eggs
Paintbrush
Paints
Brush
PVA glue

1 Boil the eggs for 10 minutes until hard. Then cool them in cold water for another ten minutes

2 Draw your design on the shell covering the whole egg.

3 Place the egg in an egg cup and carefully paint the design. When the paint is dry, turn the egg the other way and paint the other half. Leave it to dry.

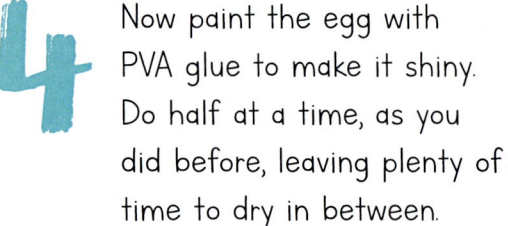

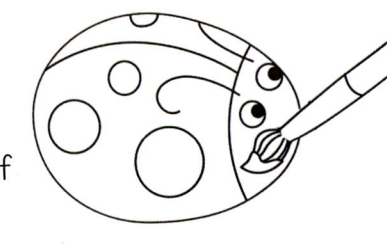

4 Now paint the egg with PVA glue to make it shiny. Do half at a time, as you did before, leaving plenty of time to dry in between.

21 Make a line of ducks

You will need
Yellow card
Brown card
Orange card
Pens
Scissors
Glue
A kitchen roll tube

1 Draw a duckling on the yellow card. Cut it out.

Draw round it three more times to get ducklings that are all the same. Cut them out.

2 Colour in the beaks and draw an eye.

3 Draw four wings on the yellow card and cut them out. Snip the edge to make a feathery effect and bend them up.

Glue them onto the ducklings.

4 Make the duck in the same way but with the brown card. Make her much bigger. Stick a bit of orange card on her beak.

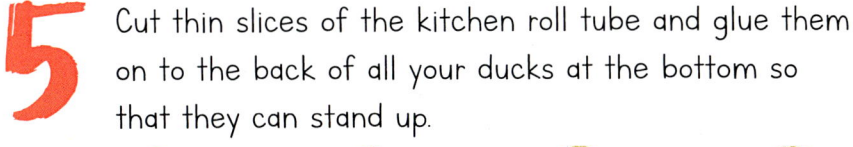

5 Cut thin slices of the kitchen roll tube and glue them on to the back of all your ducks at the bottom so that they can stand up.

35

22 Make a fluffy chick

You will need
Cardboard
Yoghurt pot to draw around
A small coin
Scissors
Yellow wool
PVA glue
Coloured paper

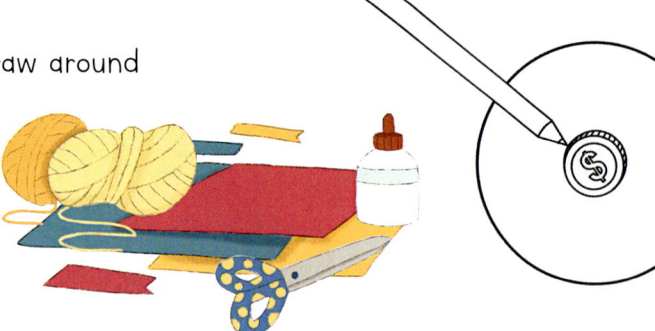

1 Draw two circles on the cardboard by drawing round the yoghurt pot. Cut them out.

Now draw two smaller circles in the middle of the larger ones by drawing round the coin. Cut them out.

2 Cut a long piece of wool and thread it through the hole to tie the two circles together.

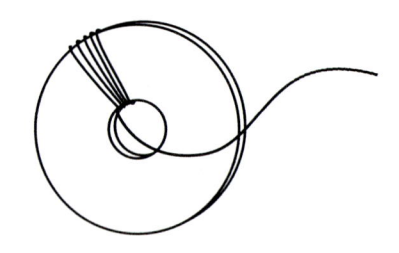

3 Keep threading it through and winding it round, so that you cover the card. If you run out of wool just tie on another bit.

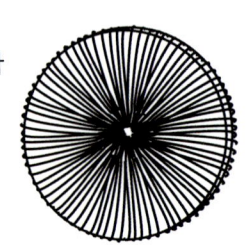

Keep going until it's really difficult to push the wool through the centre hole.

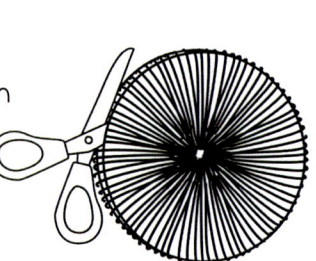

4 Put the scissors in and try to find the space between the two bits of cardboard, begin cutting the wool.

When you get to the end tie a piece of wool tightly between the cardboard circles, so that the wool is held firmly in the middle.

5 Cut away the cardboard and fluff up your chick.

6 Cut out some paper eyes and an orange beak and then stick them on.

37

23 Make a Nest for Your Chick

You will need
A small bowl
Cling film
PVA glue
Brush
A ball of brown wool or string.

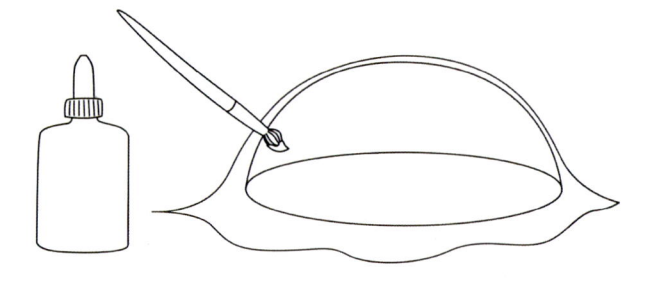

1 Turn the bowl upside down and cover it with the cling film. Brush lots of glue all over the bowl.

2 Take the end of the string and start winding it around the bowl. Start at the base and go round and round until you have covered all the glue with a layer of string.

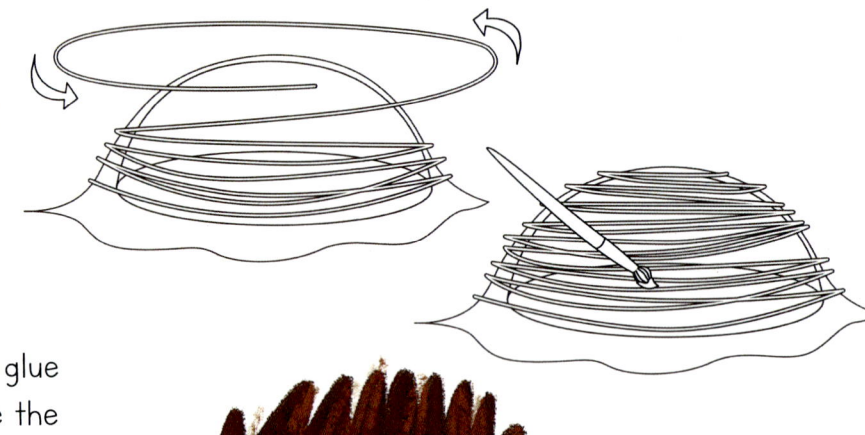

3 Brush on another layer of glue and keep going. Make sure the string soaks up the glue. Keep going until you have covered the bowl with at least two layers of string. Leave it to dry.

4 You will know when it's dry because all the glue will be see-through. Gently take it off the bowl and remove the cling film.

24 Make a hatching chick

You will need
- Some white and yellow card
- Scissors
- A paper fastener
- Pen
- Pencil
- Tape

1 Draw an egg shape onto the white card and cut it out.

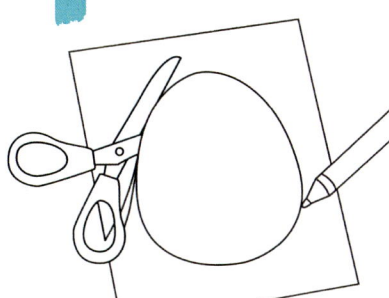

2 Cut it in half with a zig-zagging line.

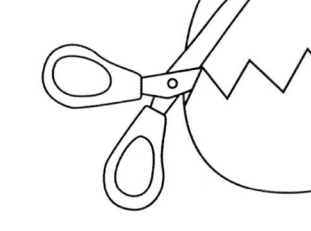

3 Draw the top half of a chick onto the yellow card.

4 Tape it onto the back of the bottom half of your egg so that the chick's head is poking out of the top.

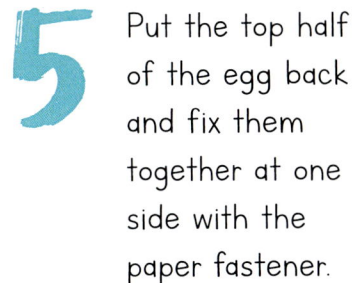

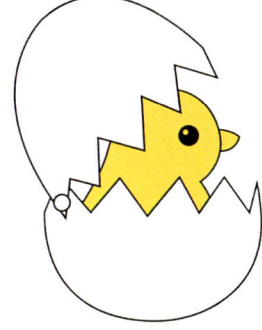

5 Put the top half of the egg back and fix them together at one side with the paper fastener.

Now you can open and shut your egg.

25 Make a flying bird

You will need
Coloured card
Coloured paper
Scissors
Sticky tape

1 Take a piece of card about 12 cm x 15 cm. Fold it in half lengthways.

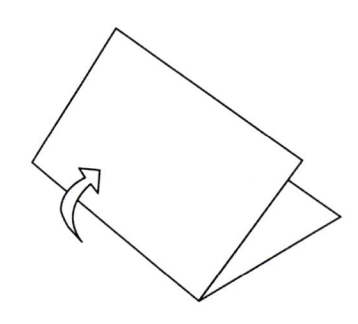

2 Draw a bird on one side using the fold as the bird's back.

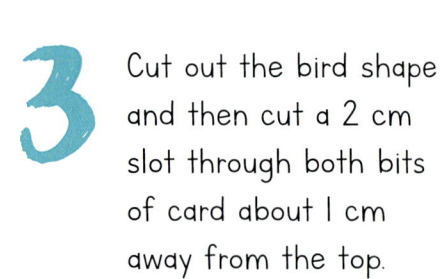

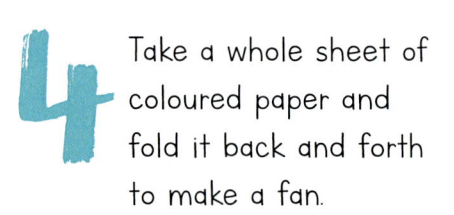

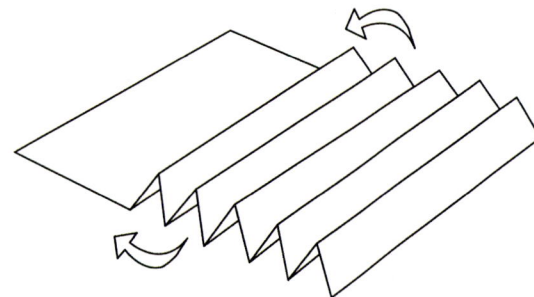

3 Cut out the bird shape and then cut a 2 cm slot through both bits of card about 1 cm away from the top.

4 Take a whole sheet of coloured paper and fold it back and forth to make a fan.

40

5 Push the fan through the slot.

When you get to the middle, fold it in half upwards. Spread out the fan to make wings.

6 To make a tail, use a piece of coloured paper about 10 cm x 5 cm.

Fold it backwards and forwards to make a fan shape.

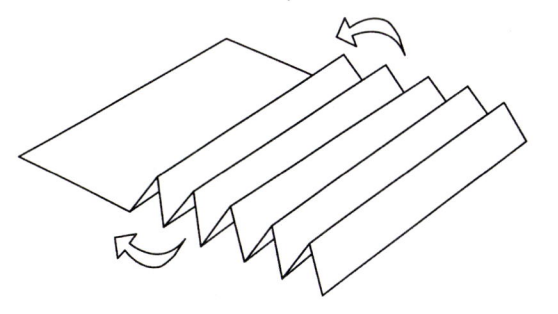

Stick one end of the fan to the inside of the bird with tape.

Gently open the paper to make the tail fan out.

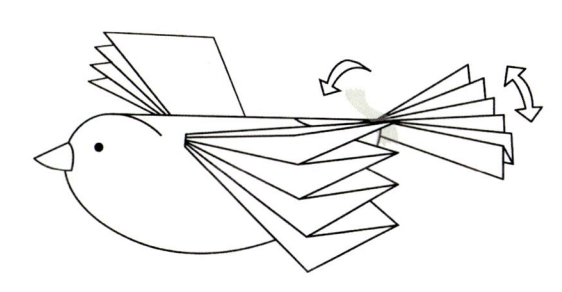

41

26 Make a Peacock

You will need
Coloured paper
Scissors
Glue stick
Pens

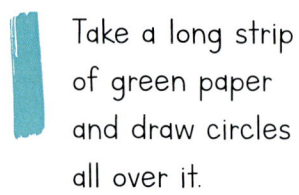

1 Take a long strip of green paper and draw circles all over it.

2 Fold it back and forth to make a fan.

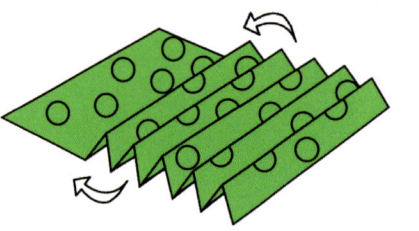

3 To make the body, draw a bird shape onto the blue paper. Draw on some feathers and then cut it with an extra strip at the back so that you can stick it onto the fan shape.

4 Fold the fan in half, open it up a little and then stick the body into the middle.

Once it's dry, spread out the fan.

27 Make a bird mobile

You will need
Two sticks
Stiff paper
Coloured pens or crayons
String
Needle and thread

1 Fold the paper in half and draw half a bird. This way the bird will be the same shape on each side. Make sure the body is next to the fold. Cut it out.

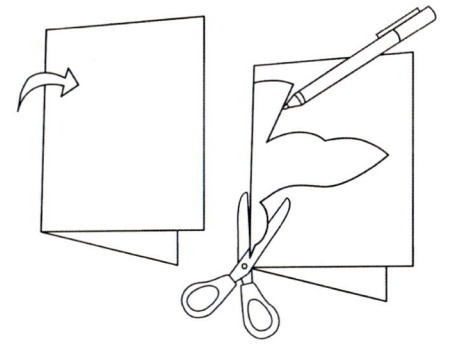

2 Open it up and colour it in on both sides.

Make four birds in the same way.

3 Tie the two sticks together in the middle to form a cross. Leave a long bit of string at the end so that you can hang it up.

4 Thread the needle and tie a knot in the end of the thread. Push the needle through the back of the bird and tie the thread to the end of one stick.

Do this three more times and hang up your mobile.

43

28 Make a curly bird

You will need
Coloured paper
Scissors
Glue

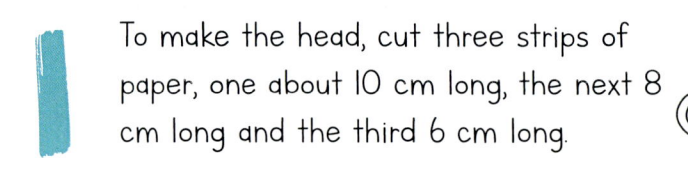

1 To make the head, cut three strips of paper, one about 10 cm long, the next 8 cm long and the third 6 cm long.

2 Stick them together at one end, and then roll them around a pencil.

3 Hold it tightly for a minute and let go so that it unravels a little.

4 Stick the end down and then squeeze one side together to make a beak.

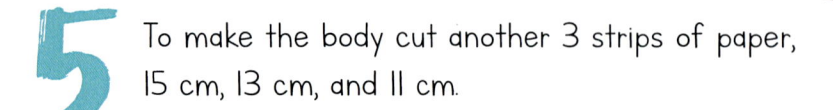

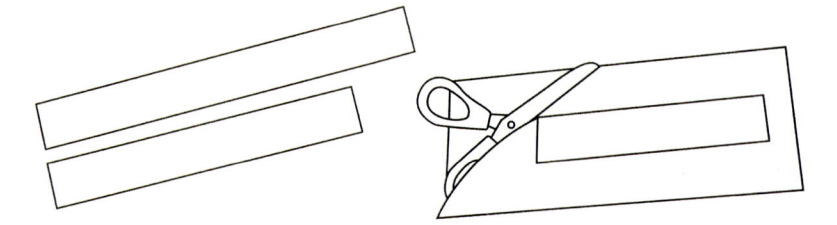

5 To make the body cut another 3 strips of paper, 15 cm, 13 cm, and 11 cm.

6 Stick them together and roll them up on the pencil like you did before and then glue the end flap down.

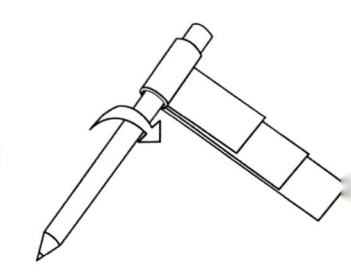

7 Now you just need the head. Cut three more strips about 8 cm, 6 cm and 4 cm long. Snip the ends so they look like feathers.

8 Now stick them together at the end and curl them up a little.

Finally, glue the body to the tail and then add the head to the body.

45

29 Make Swimming Swans

You will need
White paper sheets
Blue paint
Brush
Scissors
Glue stick
Pens

1 First paint a blue swirly picture of water on the sheet of paper. Leave it to dry.

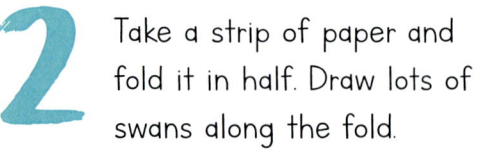

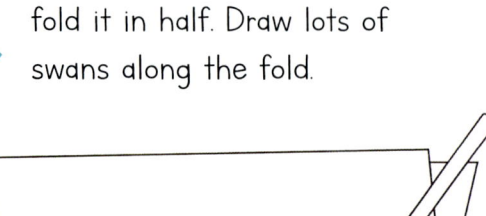

2 Take a strip of paper and fold it in half. Draw lots of swans along the fold.

3 Cut them out so that you have two birds stuck together. Colour in the eyes and beaks.

4 Stick one half of the birds onto the paper to make a family of swans swimming across the pond.

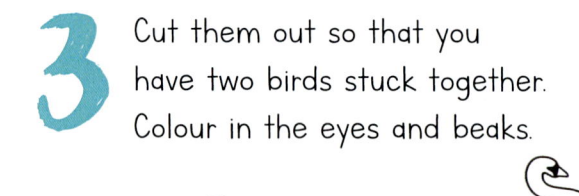

46

30 Make a Rocking Penguin

You will need

A paper cup
Pens
Black paint
Orange card
Black paper
Scissors
Glue

1 Using the orange card, draw round the bottom of the cup. Then draw some feet and two tabs on either side like the ones in the picture. Cut them out.

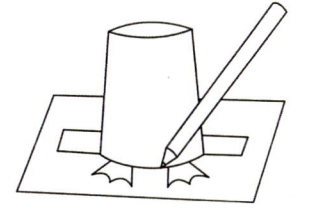

2 Draw a penguin face and body on the cup. Paint all the rest of the cup with black paint. Leave it to dry.

3 Cut two wings out of the black paper. Glue them to the side of the penguin and bend them up a bit.

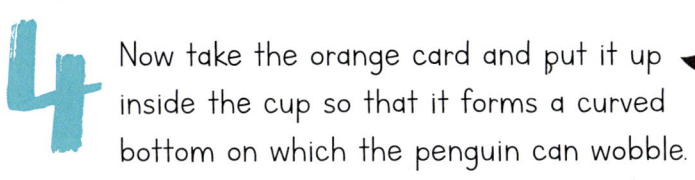

4 Now take the orange card and put it up inside the cup so that it forms a curved bottom on which the penguin can wobble.

WRITTEN BY: FELICIA LAW and LUCY BRIGNALL

EDUCATIONAL TEXT: AIMÉE JACKSON

DESIGN: FELICIA LAW and IMRAN KELLY

COLOUR ILLUSTRATIONS: MARTINA ROTONDO

BLACK LINE ILLUSTRATIONS: KERI GREEN (BEEHIVE ILLUSTRATION AGENCY)

COPYRIGHT © 2021 BrambleKids Ltd

ISBN: 978-1-914411-48-9